even god loves america

christian del pino

www.christiandelpino.com

nous croyons en dieu

je veux la vraie liberté pour sauver cette nation

in god we trust

i want real freedom to save this nation

the news is becoming even more frightening
so i tend to look away
i don't want to know about the shootings
or the nuclear meteor that almost hit us today

i would much rather ignore it
they say
ignorance brings peace
instead of having to watch the destruction
all over the half imagined news
or the burning of our trees

experts say pretty soon
there won't be enough air
for us to breathe
but somehow we continue
filling up our atmosphere
with more heat lying underneath

time is running out

to save ourselves
to save our planet

time is running out

global warming and climate change are the same tragedy

i turn on the television set
a shooting airing through the news
they say they have shot the threat
the killer must of had the blues
i say we should focus on the state of mind
of those we allow to roam around with guns
rather we just review all of the lines drawn in blood
when they start shooting we all start to run

gun control

they say it is the denouement of our world
everything we know is coming to an end
i only want to make art
is this life just pretend

these wars overseas
do they know they are fighting for me

god bless america

our mother earth is getting hot
we have become both the virus and the infection
so many of us not doing enough
destroying this earth for future generations

our planet is melting
and all we are doing is adding more steam
what can i do to stop this please tell me
will they pay attention if i post it on the livestream

so much violence
from so many guns
we must of all grown numb
you can find me here praying for everyone

sometimes i wonder if it is all of the pollution
in the skies
what else is to blame
for the taking of these innocent lives
who else is to blame
for all of these tumultuous trying times

i wrote some poetry about
some recent shootings airing on the news
but since then we have had
some more shootings or was it thirty two more
some are getting scared
others going mad
terrified really for their own lives
i don't want to live in a country
where some can't even go outside

some but mostly black

so much plastic in our oceans
the fish can't get around
the fish can't swim

so much toxic gas in the atmosphere above us
we can't seem to figure it out
soon we won't be able to live

i miss los angeles
and the america my father remembers
i have so much but i really want less
i just want my words to be remembered

the sun sets so beautifully on this side of our earth
the sun sets so differently on this side of our earth

it must be all of the
gun smoke
gentrification
hunger
and inequality

the sun sets so beautifully on america
the sun sets so differently on america

we have it all but seem to do nothing

we are all born woman
with nipple to represent the transition
we all experience in the womb
we are all born greatness
we are all born equal
we are all born woman

our amazon rainforest
is turning into ash
we are creating sculptures of plastic
we are just creating piles of trash

the glaciers at the tips of our planet
are turning into sea
those who study our world and our climate
say time is running out just wait and see

climate change is real

this land of ours did not place its first settlers into camps
as they tried and searched for a better life
why must we do it now to those who try and cross
can someone please shed some light

we are all immigrants

our world is driving itself mad
countries not respecting the privacy of man
have we gone back in time
fashion
records
and politics
it almost feels like a fad are we all just scared
i am calling my dad

i have said it before our world is burning
it is us humans making it this damn hot
but we don't give it a second damn thought
we should take better notes from our ancestors
reimagine everything we were ever taught
wars upon wars
is this really all we know
there are more wars needing to be fought

our earth is crying
in need of someone to tend
how can we stop these countries from fighting
i have a few words to lend
if we do not change our ways now
we may soon be found without a planet to defend

now

christian del pino

to care for our earth
we must first begin to care for our waters

our oceans are drowning

our president is mad
i am scared for my life
these wars are rampant
what is this talk about nuclear vice

we are all drowning
from every corner of this world
can we ban together
can we put out the fires
can we end the wars overseas
i still have hope for this world
it is all i could see

trump i

what kind of america is this
we cannot trust the president
with our lives
we cannot trust the president
with his lies

trump ii

nothing in my generation
lasts longer than six seconds
am i still a lover of this freedom nation
but what about all of the shootings going on in texas

everyone around me
aimlessly walking with their heads down
maybe watching a livestream
or shooting photos of the ground

i'll write the poetry to fit in their little screens
maybe scribble in a little tree
calming the darker screams
the ones they can relate to
the poetry they can see

they interrupted the post with breaking news
another shooting today but this is nothing new
they say the victim was killed because he was gay
his parents are mourning
why
they exclaim it is getting way too real
let's wait for something new in the morning

the six second news

it is only screens now everywhere i look
whether i am out for a drive
or in the middle of the woods

fahrenheit 451

i have trouble staying present in the moment
always finding myself thinking ahead
when a good thing happens
i am always wondering what's next
and then when it comes and it goes
i regret not being able to cherish
the moments i am slowly letting go
all of it waiting for me to perish

i still worry i won't get out of life
what i have been feverishly working to spend
so i write melancholic poetry about america
thinking about the end

i want the worry
to melt off of my skin
the same way you left
and on a cellular level
i haven't been the same since

thoughts of you and the suicidal ones
together they string themselves into one
a continuous nightmare another closed door
who am i really writing all of this poetry for

sometimes
we get so stuck within the walls of our own minds
we forget the simplicity in just living our lives

i fear watching my mother
and my father grow old
i fear the lessons they told
are the ones i never learned

will we have enough time together

vintage flashbacks of woodstock on the walls
you want all of me and i give you nothing at all

i moved into the city
and found a river near my flat
i spent many nights here watching the boats drive passed
while i contemplated sweet jazz

a few boats near the dock
and the moon in its full bloom
a halo of light surrounding the rock
it is so bright in this room

i trek my way back home
while i conjure up another poem
i have spent so much time writing them into books
i want to spend the rest of my life writing them for you

vintage abandoned cars under tired streets lamps
remind me of the way he left
i write the poetry to soothe my aching heart
but sometimes it is just so sad

maybe i am too small to change the world
poetry lost in libraries
a quiet voice amongst the crowd
how i wish things were different
how i wish this lifetime wasn't so hard

i miss the vintage american
dead malls in the middle of california
i want to write the vintage american
poetry of us in the middle of california

i can see mountains in your eyes
and across the bay
i live for the days you look into my eyes
we stay at bay

i miss the city streets and the pawn stops
in the middle of california
we drive to san jose just a few more stops
i miss loving you in the middle of california

i tend to stay dead for you
knowing if i woke up i would run
i tell you it was all for you
but i know everything is always my fault

i was thousands of miles away
lost somewhere deep in the california state
you wanted me near but i didn't want to stay
so i left california and you decided it was too late

lost lover

you blamed me for all of the fires
in california

i blamed you for all of the fires
deep inside of my heart

you said loving me was like living
in the dark

maybe it was my fault

we always want more
until the more
is not enough anymore

i let you inside
allowed you to build a home
out of wood and nail

what do you mean
you are leaving

we went to war against each other
none of us made it out
alive

turn up the folk record
i am transcending passed the troubles of this generation
it is all too much and i can't seem to take it

are you good at dying because i am the master
i do it every single night with intention
i must be a bastard

i listen to the cries of my ancestors
in hopes of a clue or racial backlash
white
white
white
everything white
and enough mint candles to burn america down

cry me the entire mississippi river
watch me drown

my ancestors were slaves so i do it for them

daddy i almost had to kill you
leaving me in the atlantic
feeling blue blue blue
we were merely a ship a sinking titanic
the sky painted blue blue blue
when you are not here
i can only think of you you you

homage to sylvia plath

my heartbeat quickens
a year following the trauma
the honeysuckle on my lip thickens
let's go away to waimea

i just want to make some mediocre art
this life is just too much
you have a habit of taking it too damn far
i miss loving you and your distant touch

my vision blurs
a year after the trauma
i see myself laying in a hearse
is this some sort of karma

life is a bowl of cherries

i am placing the cathode ray tube on static
turning the radio transmission set in between
two different frequencies
opening every window and letting in the sun
then i will read to you the poems
i have written before dawn

early mourning ritual

white walls lined in stone i am seeing ghosts
along my home
they share your characteristics
they look like you and speak loud
i paint myself in pure violet
filling up the tub in hopes that i drown
i am scared to walk around
they are everywhere
nowhere
up and
down

i clean the wooden floorboards
and the table we would sit at too
this used to be my home
but that was until i met you

i am still trying to wash away your memory

i moved to california thinking i could find myself
somewhere near yosemite
or along the boardwalk of the famous santa cruz
i traveled through to los angeles
but here i only found the blues
i flew all the way to san jose
and ended up halfway into monterey
so i thought i would look for myself there
and as soon as i started feeling better
it all just went to hell
so i decided to hike up to palo alto
and ended up near san francisco
i tried looking for myself again here
but what i found i didn't bring near

a steep hike through california

you are a storm of wants

a cup of burnt coffee
and a small silver spoon
you want to leave me
i have nothing more to do

pouring rain on this side of miami
the sky must know you don't want me
grey clouds and no sign of the sun
maybe i will love you forever maybe you are the only one

the city lights beam
everything painted in heavy neon green
i wonder if god can feel me suffer
it's getting hot you were always such a lousy lover

i have learned so much
from the unloving of you

how could i not see it before
you were poisoned tips painted black
i saw you walk out the door
i hope you never come back

there are waves in your eyes
and i seem to be drowning alive

i am grateful for the love
i am grateful for the loss
i am grateful for you
the most of all

the greatest
homage to elizabeth woolridge grant

i will sail the seven seas
just tell me where to flee
i want to get away
from everything you have ever done to me

sailor

thinking about you is a dead end

what corner of my room do i turn into
when i miss you and you aren't here

i miss the california sun
but i miss you more
did you run out of love
for you i will wait by the door

i miss sitting with you by the yard outside
by the trees and our proclaimed lake
you told me to catch you on the flipside
it seems disappearing was your greatest trait

how has los angeles treated you since i left
do you still drive down the same dirt road we rode
or do you take the side streets lined in green palm trees

i remember when we had everything
we had each other what more could we want
we had everything in the grasp of our hands
but all of it is long gone

the city of angels

just the mere thought of you
and i melt
into a sea of anxiety

i grew tired of waiting for you
the flower petals along my arms drooped

tainted soil

i laid awake through so many
sleepless nights
trying to get the look of your eyes
out of mine

it pains me to not have you here

i am but a poet without a muse
norman rockwell without the blues
devastation without the news

it hurts me not having you here
anymore

our veins would dance around each other
almost as if they were running towards the same heart

we had everything why did you decide to leave me here

do you think we blamed one another
because we were both afraid
of the same demon

i cannot seem to figure out if
the poetry is either healing
or hurting

pain is pain is loneliness

i think about the spring
those flowers that grow with thorns
how the sun still shines
after each and every storm

i still think about how much i have grown
since we saw each other near those trees
how i still rise like a mountain
after i am brought down to my knees

birds across the sky blue
learning to see a deeper you
clouds and street lamps dampen my view
learning to forget you

we must be living on the sun
watching each other burn are we already dead
it has always been my fault my love hasn't it
i am learning to quiet the voices in my head

they tell me i should not trust you

you hold me close
i am learning to count the constellations in your eyes
you learn to hide the deepest
the bluest
parts of you
i have always been wearing a disguise

afraid

glass windows overlooking the garden of peaches
from the wooden floors to the golden roof
i don't want any of this
if i can't have you

mid century bridges and perfectly aged yachts
around the river with mansions in half golden
the other half silver locks
gargoyles near the bronze gate
you are an ocean of self hate
you are synonymous for leaving around the spring
you tell me it is because your patience
has been wearing thin
man child i
or man child you
you tell me you really love me
is anything you say really true

summers by the marina

i still wear you
like ripped clothing

this room needs more flowers

in my head

you taste like that of pure freedom
unsifted liberty with the ruthless aftertaste of
pacific ocean
sometimes you are rough but i have learned to navigate
your emotions

catching the reflection of the sun
are you my one and only one
the rays keep getting hot
please don't make me wait so long

how am i not to be grateful
for this seemingly perfect life
we are just consuming we are being so wasteful
let's drown by the high tides

you explain how you'd be right back
just another minute i'm burning up
we go where we know into a familiar track
i need more coffee to fill up my cup

i loved you so much but you never seemed to love me back

melted bicycles chained to telephone poles
you loved me when i didn't love me

my depression ruined us both

a love so virtual
some say it is nonexistent
you call me sweet candy names
but i have never been listening

y2k i

the mundane back and forth
of your place or mine
this love tastes bland
you call it summer wine

y2k ii

the last time you came back
my skin melted off of my body
my mind disappeared and left no sign of existence
my heart pumped liquid nitrogen through my skeleton

this was when i knew
my body wanted nothing more
to do with you

the ulcers inside of my mouth
have multiplied

i miss you

i have not heard from you
in months
do you still have the blues
how did i ever lose your trust

maybe this is a good thing
you have been so distant
i still call your name in hopes you are listening
maybe by next christmas

i have not heard from you
in years
did you find someone new to choose
did you conquer those paralyzing fears

the wounds of our heartbreak still sting
the memories of you are calling and i am missing
i pray by the ocean listening to del rey sing
i think of your impeccable smile and how it would glisten

i have not heard from you
in a decade
have the memories of you and i started to fade
it has been an entire lifetime but here i will stay

where i stand vines have begun to grow
gardens have come but they said they had to go
my feet are now stuck to the concrete
i tell them *just wait and see*
you'll be back where did you go have you thought of me

it is physical
the pain
your loss
it is physical

the waves are getting higher
my hopes are sinking low
i know i know i know
this will never work out
but you know i never trust in my soul

reprise from the rain
2015

what do the thoughts of you
survive off of

i swear i go weeks and months
without a single memory of us
and out of nowhere
i am brought right back to your feet in prayer
asking the universe what i can do
to make you mine again

upon the twenty fifth rotation around the sun
you are still the one i love
i miss my brother and how i miss my mom
and the life we once lived
but we grew older
and i stopped believing in god
then this world hit me like a boulder

i imagined a life filled to the brim in subconscious poetry
you woke me from the dream a little too early
i spent my lucid morning thinking of you and this country
and the generation i wanted you and i to become
you ask me *what is the hurry*
i cry and scream *this world is burning*
and so came my anxiety
it is something we cannot fix with all of our printed money

wake me up upon the twenty sixth rotation around the sun
i give to you my everything
but i will always get your nothing at all

toxicity turns hearts into rust

am i a glass of rose water
or a lake filled with blood

was it my fault

you make your way back into my life
almost as if you had an intention to stay
almost as if you had left something
the last time you stopped by

what did you forget this time
was it the last string of my heart

even after all of this time
i let you back in
almost as if it was me who forgot to tell you something
the last time you came in

three story homes down paradise way
we lost ourselves on the strip
but i loved you along the way

boulders and rocks at almost every turn
you come and you go we're not coheres
does my disappearing act still haunt you
i bet my pain was worse

some time in nevada

i spent some time in the silver state
you take me to downtown las vegas
so we try not to stay out so late
wishing someone would save us

a heavy drive out of the city
we play some sad records and reconcile our past
you tell me it's easy living
i tell you without you i still get trashed

we drive up to the canyon
i get lost in the heat
i write you another poem
this one claiming my defeat

time zones through arizona and red rocks
vintage american dam stops
some plath poetry to pass the time
but you tell me you'd rather read mine

should we go to la or san jose
the suicidal thoughts start trickling fast
we play some rubber soul to soothe the pain
look at how quickly they go away then come back

journey

loneliness is a powerful sin
it turns me against myself
it always lets you win

it is not going to last forever
it is not going to last forever
it is not going to last forever
it is not going to last forever
it is not going to last forever
it is not going to last forever
it is not going to last forever
it is not going to last forever
it is not going to last forever
it is not going to last forever
it is not going to last forever
it is not going to last forever
it is not going to last forever
it is not going to last forever
it is not going to last forever
it is not going to last forever
it is not going to last forever
it is not going to last forever
it is not going to last forever
it is not going to last forever
it is not going to last forever
it is not going to last forever
it is not going to last forever
it is not going to last forever
it is not going to last forever
it is not going to last forever
it is not going to last forever
it is not going to last forever
it is not going to last forever
it is not going to last forever
it is not going to last forever
it is not going to last forever
it is not going to last forever
it is not going to last forever

the pain

you had no intentions of staying
and i didn't realize it until
the dandelions i had planted along your chest
bloomed
then beheaded themselves

the inspiration walked away with you

90

i feel drained lifeless and half insane
i gave it all up it is now art around a frame
it has a small description to the bottom right and my name
i think i lost myself along the way

across art galleries

let the waters rush in
i am ready

i keep meeting you
in hopes i find a version of you
willing to stay

am i enough or will i ever be
i only wanted you but you wanted to leave
maybe god after all doesn't really love me

i let a little more of you go yesterday

i woke up this morning shining with so much
self love you can see it from the moon

if i loved you the way you loved me
there wouldn't be much left of you

at the end of us
i found the beginning of myself

i am finished with this body
i am putting a *for sale* sign across my chest
offering it up to the lowest bidder
this one comes with defects

you have lived without him this long haven't you

survival mechanism

be your own summer solstice

it is so easy to give up
but to keep believing in yourself
when no one else does
takes magic

the darkness is powerful
isn't it
how i can have all of the rivieras
this mediocre world has to offer
yet
the darkness reminds me
just how small i really am
just how unworthy i really am
just how sad i really am
without you here with me

if the rain has taught me anything
it is that i can either
drown in the puddle
or dance in it

even rain offers life

your distance made it easy to leave

the day you left i cried
until my eyes confused themselves
for clouds
wondering how i held
so much water underneath my eyelids

eventually the thoughts of you
starved themselves into
nothing

give yourself the opportunity to grieve
what has been lost

give yourself the opportunity to feel
what is to come

today i am learning how to live without you
all over again

it is possible to heal from the trauma
it is possible to heal from the trauma
it is possible to heal from the trauma
it is possible to heal from the trauma
it is possible to heal from the trauma
it is possible to heal from the trauma
it is possible to heal from the trauma
it is possible to heal from the trauma
it is possible to heal from the trauma
it is possible to heal from the trauma
it is possible to heal from the trauma
it is possible to heal from the trauma
it is possible to heal from the trauma
it is possible to heal from the trauma
it is possible to heal from the trauma
it is possible to heal from the trauma
it is possible to heal from the trauma
it is possible to heal from the trauma
it is possible to heal from the trauma
it is possible to heal from the trauma
it is possible to heal from the trauma
it is possible to heal from the trauma
it is possible to heal from the trauma
it is possible to heal from the trauma
it is possible to heal from the trauma
it is possible to heal from the trauma
it is possible to heal from the trauma
it is possible to heal from the trauma
it is possible to heal from the trauma
it is possible to heal from the trauma
it is possible to heal from the trauma
it is possible to heal from the trauma
it is possible to heal from the trauma

i miss the innocence of youth

i want to be full like the moon

i am not afraid of death anymore

this happened long after i realized
i have been dead before
i have died a few times already
and i will die at the end of this lifetime

compassion
the very first ingredient in self love

keep your glass of water
i carry oceans inside of me

i want to write myself a thousand love letters

he doesn't have the same taste
your lips have
i am still trying to figure out
whether this is good or bad

new love

christian del pino

you taste like the sun
i am in flames

i wanted to write you a love poem
about the way my eyes confuse you for the sun

i wanted to write you another love poem
but all i could think about was the way your eyes
reflect the light of the sun

i wanted to write about the way you love me
but all i could think about was the way you hold me
as if i was all that existed in the middle of the night

i wanted to write about how your smile
is all i seem to think about when you are not here
how i want all of you forever
wondering if this is all a dream

lover

everything before you was pure darkness
everything before you just didn't make sense
everything before you was suffocating black but now
it is like i can breathe

everything now feels like summer
i have spent so much time waiting for you to arrive
now it feels like i am home

the stars have been preparing me
only my entire life
to bring you to me

i have finally found you
what else do i need

with you i have struck gold
i found the golden ticket in the lottery of love
no need to look any further
you fit like my favorite glove
go on and ask my father
you are unlike anyone

will you marry me

christian del pino

you tell me we will be together forever
but my love what *forever* can you promise
if you and i must one day die

will we promise to pick up
right where we left off
together in our next lifetime

forever

you love everything about me i seem to hate
you are sweet like cherry pie
you sing me to sleep like a soothing lullaby
you bring me down when i am too much inside of my head
you ease the pain of trying to forget those who left

i daydream about my childhood
and the worry i never seemed to have had
you make me grateful to be alive
i stopped feeling so sad

i understand you aren't so much into poetry
hurry along it is time for you to go to work
drive safe and think of me as you pass that old oak tree
i will stay inside and write you another book

forever seems so far away

but seconds
when i am with you

you turn honey
sweet
less

natural sweetener

you explain to me how difficult it is
for you to show your love and affection
to tell me just how you really feel

but my love i can hear it in the way you smile
when you look at me as we drive through the canyon

i can see it when you tell me to be careful
or to watch my step

i can feel it when your lips touch mine

i can hear your silence

when did i get this lucky
to have met you in total darkness
this is nothing short of a miracle

love light

i do not even think about you anymore
ever since i met him
your taste
your touch
your eyes
they seem to have faded
like my childhood memories

i do not even write about you anymore
not since i started loving him
your violence
your hands
those eyes
they don't seem to have the same side effects
on me anymore

ever since i found him
i forgot that we ever existed

the hells of hell
were worth the fire
as you emerged from the other side
my life only got brighter

it is not you but on some nights
you drown me in love i feel i do not deserve
i let the sadness
the trauma
the past
take over
i make a million excuses for the darkness
but then you
you come over
like an ocean wave
and paint me creamy blue

creamy blue

how have i been living
this long
without you inside of my veins

you are a dream i dream when i am awake

he loves me for who i am
wholeheartedly
and maybe
just maybe
this is enough

you take the poetry
out of my lips

with you
what is there to be afraid of

this love i feel for you is older than we are

we are endless

i want to be in between
where you start
and i finish

when you hold me
my heart sinks into everlasting calmness
every worry
gone
every regret
gone
every reason to ever let go
gone

i now know why they fought wars
for a love like ours

when i am not with you
it is almost as if i couldn't breathe
you are everywhere
i want to be

whether we are meditating
in the garden
or ruling the kingdom in my room
you are everything to me
graceful like the moon

i love you infinitely
i love you infinitely
i love you infinitely
i love you infinitely
i love you infinitely
i love you infinitely
i love you infinitely
i love you infinitely
i love you infinitely
i love you infinitely
i love you infinitely
i love you infinitely
i love you infinitely
i love you infinitely
i love you infinitely
i love you infinitely
i love you infinitely
i love you infinitely
i love you infinitely
i love you infinitely
i love you infinitely
i love you infinitely
i love you infinitely
i love you infinitely
i love you infinitely
i love you infinitely
i love you infinitely
i love you infinitely
i love you infinitely
i love you infinitely
i love you infinitely
i love you infinitely
i love you infinitely
i love you infinitely
i love you infinitely
i love you infinitely

your arms

paradise

this life of yours is a gift
treat it as such

you have shown me why everything before you
was a prelude
why everything before you
was complete and utter darkness

you pull the sun out of the night sky every morning
with just your smile

a shooting in california
interrupting the poems
headlining the news a few hours ago
they tell me i should spend less time writing the poetry
i tell them they don't know how much it calms me

if god can still love america
after everything we are doing to us
then i am sure god can still love me
as long as i'm either trying
or dying

in god we trust

we flip through the satellite channels
another death
but we don't flinch we never payed any mind
they say those who live must also die
and we didn't know him so we don't mind

we run through the satellite channels
another shooting
another life
he was young he was black he was gay
what change will my poetry make
living in flames and what about the laws they make

we skip through the satellite channels
they say our world is coming to an end
maybe a poem to soothe the hearts
of those who have given up on mankind
i tell you how you act so rough
you tell me i'm just too kind

even god loves america
so the hope exists for me
to love myself through the darkness
the pieces you can and cannot see

my ability to write the poetry
a privilege
living in my beautiful america
a privilege
growing old with you
a privilege
creating these pages here
a privilege
this lifetime
a privilege

all of america can love you
and this is all true
but you
you must love yourself too

maybe i should just give up on the poetry
maybe it just isn't meant to be
maybe writing the poetry for your eyes
is all it will ever be

i should just let it go
like water trickling down a waterfall
maybe i should just let go of the poetry
the same way he let go of me
it was easy for you wasn't it
to leave something you had spent so much love on
out into the wind
out of mind
out of sight
what is the point of this life anyway
if not to just waste away in space and in time

watch me say goodbye to the poetry
i am putting it all away
let america care for itself
let someone else worry about our oceans and our trees
this writing is all for nothing
watch as i leave it all behind me

swan song

you feed me liquid sugar
you say it is to quiet down the pain
my brother just got married
yesterday was his wedding day

what if none of us
really have this life thing figured out
a forest fire in the distance
will you ever love me right

i want to become a poet for my generation
but what poetry can i write for you when all i am being fed
is political distress and war presence
i want to live more
in the present moment practicing meditation
all i know about love is my parent's lousy marriage

driving down alligator alley
in someone else's car but we are almost home
watching the trees pass us by i have never been this happy
it has been such a dark year but look
at how much you've grown

did we forget about the burning trees
in our beautiful rainforests
is it because we replaced the news
with more shootings
or another historical tweet
i love this country of mine
but sometimes i just want to be free

freedom comes at a cost

i look at you
and every poem
every lyric
every war over love
just makes sense

i convinced myself love was out of the question
i would never find it
it would never find me

but this was until you walked into my life
out of thin air
like a dream
like a daydream

i have never felt more awake
i have never felt more alive
or more deserving of your golden heart

for erik

i run to you almost as if the sun didn't exist

you remind me of the sun in the spring
this is the universe forgiving all of my sin

you are a clear blue sky
you make me grateful for this precious life

you are the ocean so lively and pure
you remind me why it never worked
with anyone else before

i want to spend the rest of my life
next to you
writing out the poetry of our lives
scribed with ink onto the volumes of books
we will write together

you are the poem

how can i possibly
grow impatient
we have only
the rest of our lives
together

it is all different with you
it is like night and day
like life and death
like love and pain

it is all different with you
than it was with him

i cannot help but compare

christian del pino

let me spend the rest of my life
giving you the same happiness
you have given me

a love poem

you are full of magic
you are full of magic
you are full of magic
you are full of magic
you are full of magic
you are full of magic
you are full of magic
you are full of magic
you are full of magic
you are full of magic
you are full of magic
you are full of magic
you are full of magic
you are full of magic
you are full of magic
you are full of magic
you are full of magic
you are full of magic
you are full of magic
you are full of magic
you are full of magic
you are full of magic
you are full of magic
you are full of magic
you are full of magic
you are full of magic
you are full of magic
you are full of magic
you are full of magic
you are full of magic

i do not know what is to come
once this lifetime is over
i can only hope
i can only pray
the next lifetime still has you in it

you fight for your life
from the second you welcome in the new day
like a soldier woken from the bunkers
with the sounds of explosions from far away

i am not sure how you do it
high then low
low then high
high then low
low then high
i am not sure how you do it

something many of us take for granted
turning sweetness into poison
turning grapes into wine
turning morning into night

diabetes

driving in the car through the canyon
our fingertips must of been dipped in raw honey
the sun is beaming through the glass on the roof
as we exist in pure love

you wrote this poem

the trauma returns in the middle of the night
when it is late and my mind begins to list off
all of the reasons you would be better off without me
and so i plot against myself
the self sabotage
a familiar feeling
a dark hole
that is until i look at you
and you remind me that you love me
always and unconditionally
and the worry washes away
like sand along the coast
and i am brought right back
here
with you
in your arms
with my body
in your eyes
tasting honey

i am done with the self sabotage

bring on the self love

i want to shine with so much self love
the sun turns its head in jealousy

never give up on your dreams
they are what feed you
they are what keep you
alive

some days i still get anxious

some days i am still brought back to the darkness
but then i meditate on my progress

my growth
where i am

what i have accomplished
those i have had the honor of impacting

those who have impacted me

i think about giving up on myself
but remember the kingdom i have built inside of my chest

i have spent far too many late nights and early mornings
chiseling away at myself

inching away at the porcelain
to see it all crumble over a temporary mood

i am writing myself a love letter

for all of the times i told myself i wasn't enough
for all of the times i did not believe i could
for all of the times i let my mind take control
for all of the times i was not patient with myself

i am writing myself a love letter
because who else can love me
the way i love me

i am writing myself a love letter
because i am all that i have
because i am all that i need

i wrote myself a love letter

let them say what they want to say
at the end of the day
they will say what they want to say
but when i look into your eyes
it is like looking into the sun
as long as i love you
nothing else comes close to being enough

it should not be so taboo
for a same sex couple
to walk down the street holding hands

it should not be so dangerous
for a same sex couple
to walk down the street holding hands

fear of reprisal

i wanted to give thanks
to those who came before me
who crawled through hate speeches
so that i may walk in parades
or public spaces with
the man i call the love of my life

i wanted to give thanks
to all of those who fought the wars against
those opposed to homosexuality
and lost their lives
so that i may marry
the man i call the love of my life

i wanted to say thank you
to everyone who has died under chains
of oppression and resistance
so that i may live happily and free with
the man i call the love of my life

gay rights are human rights

would you prefer silver chains
around my arms and throat
no
i will use this tongue and my words
to speak into ears who i have become

i need to spend less time
focusing on this world
and what they think of me
and the poems

i need to spend more time
focusing on me
and on the poems

investment

your words taste like thorns
with poisoned tips
i bleed
you see me as un
human
while i am having to force myself
to just see myself as alive

if i left it up to you
i would be gone by now
but i am leaving it up to me
and i want to live
forever

do not judge your own progress in the process
do not judge your own progress in the process
do not judge your own progress in the process
do not judge your own progress in the process
do not judge your own progress in the process
do not judge your own progress in the process
do not judge your own progress in the process
do not judge your own progress in the process
do not judge your own progress in the process
do not judge your own progress in the process
do not judge your own progress in the process
do not judge your own progress in the process
do not judge your own progress in the process
do not judge your own progress in the process
do not judge your own progress in the process
do not judge your own progress in the process
do not judge your own progress in the process
do not judge your own progress in the process
do not judge your own progress in the process
do not judge your own progress in the process
do not judge your own progress in the process
do not judge your own progress in the process
do not judge your own progress in the process
do not judge your own progress in the process
do not judge your own progress in the process
do not judge your own progress in the process
do not judge your own progress in the process
do not judge your own progress in the process
do not judge your own progress in the process
do not judge your own progress in the process
do not judge your own progress in the process
do not judge your own progress in the process
do not judge your own progress in the process

i pray my bones will forgive me soon
for carrying more weight than i should

i pray my lungs will forgive me soon
so much smoke i breathe in from those around me

i pray my legs will forgive me soon
i have walked miles for others
who will not take a step forward for me

i pray my heart will forgive me soon
for loving others who couldn't find it inside
to love themselves

even god loves america

i cry myself to sleep or until i drown
filling up my blood splattered bedroom walls
with gallons of salted tears
i cry myself to sleep
drowning into tomorrow
hoping i can forgive myself
for eating meat again
with a rosary clasped between my fingertips
i forgive myself
because if i cannot forgive myself
then no one ever will

rosary

write the poetry
take the photos
paint all over the canvas if you must

do not worry so much
about who is watching

so often i need to be reminded

i am exactly where i need to be
i need to trust this universe
i need to trust it is on my side
i need to trust the road i am on is the road i must take

loving someone with your same heart of gold
is the simplest form of love
but loving someone with different
opinions
values
experiences
thoughts
this
this form of love takes strength
from every nerve in your porcelain body

i had spent so many years
in complete darkness
i almost forgot
what the sun felt like on my skin

nightfall

maybe i cannot see the poetry anymore
maybe it is because
i am blinded by all of the light
in my life

daylight

we always seem to want more
until the more
never becomes enough

it was no longer streaming
on the television set
nor a photo posted online
or a livestream broadcasting from miles away

a shooting a few feet away
this hurts on a cellular level
it could have been me walking outside

it has never felt more real
or more difficult to believe
if you are reading this
please spread more peace

pray for peace

heavy metal and electronic smoke fill our lungs
what is this generation doing
we're just doing what we have been doing all along
we're all crying for help in an endless cycle of broken trust

trying to heal each other's open wounds
when we can't seem to fix ourselves first
is it safe to just be who we are
or do we lie until we make it to the hearse

we seem to be infatuated with the pain
and the side effects from the lustless love of our parents
are we just trying to become them
making ourselves completely transparent

in the history of our species
this pain has never been more real
to think we are awake but are we really dreaming
maybe it is because we aren't really prepared to feel

am i making any sense
or is this poetry all just pounding inside of my head
i am trying to save us with my measly words
but my efforts appear to be dead

twenty first century breakdown

i have let so much go
over this past year
it is like i am shedding eyelashes
of those who have caused
more harm
than good
while i am outgrowing some
i have been able to reach others

over this past year
i have learned
not to hold onto things
that want to fly
but to love
as if tomorrow i will die

over the year

i have seen so much i must have turned small

when my heart races i begin to feel unsafe
inside of my own body

and so the worried thoughts
they hurry

but i sit and write the poetry
as it all rushes away

and i can't help but stop and pray
for those who have lost their lives along the way

to the thoughts that roam inside of their minds
it is horrifying to feel as if the darkness

will never subside
but breathe

just breathe
i am right here with you

this storm will pass
and the sun will shine once again

i miss you dearly
my old friend

suicide

i am at a funeral
an open casket
a dead body
aimless conversation

i am mindlessly counting every other place
i would rather be than right here right now
wondering
if the one in the casket is thinking the same

death

we don't talk about it often enough
not enough poems about funerals

and what we feel
when we lose someone

and watch them suffocate
underneath the soil

i am sorry our world
is sometimes made out of thorn
brick and sharp nail
i am sorry we couldn't keep you here with us
long enough to watch you heal

i am so sorry you had to go

i know our thoughts are powerful
they move mountains
but sometimes they create them
and when the sun hides behind the rock
everything turns into night
all of the time
and the darkness seems to win

i am so sorry you had to go

when you find yourself here
find someone
someone you love
someone you trust
and speak
let the darkness find its way out of your throat

i am sending love
to those who believed they couldn't make it
out of the darkness alive

a note to those who took their own life

.

you are so loved

you are so loved
you are so loved

you are so loved
you are so loved

you are so loved
you are so loved

you are so loved
you are so loved

you are so loved
you are so loved

you are so loved
you are so loved

you are so loved
you are so loved

you are so loved
you are so loved

you are so loved
you are so loved

you are so loved
you are so loved

you are so loved
you are so loved

you are so loved
you are so loved

you are so loved
you are so loved

you are so loved
you are so loved

you are so loved
you are so loved

if it can happen for someone else
it can happen for you

we are all made out of magic

tie the word hope around your waist and let the ocean take you away so that hope may keep you afloat hope is what has allowed you to be here with me today hope is running through your veins and pumping blood throughout your body the hope that one day you will get passed this hope is what must allow you to never give up on yourself to feel human and overflow with love hope is the promise one day you will wake up from this thunderstorm from this nightmare and finally be able to sit on your knees and kiss the sunflowers on their petals and whisper to them how much you have missed the sun let them show you how you must have hope the bad moments will fold themselves into great nothingness let the hope fall from the moon at night and reach your skin reach your eyes let the hope allow mint to grow on your skin you are made out of pure gold you carry hope in your eyes and you see the world in color let hope keep you alive let hope carry you home when your knees have given up on themselves dip the word hope in rose water add seven tulips and let it boil then fill your tub with the elixir remove all of your clothes every single negative thought that is hung on your spine then step inside let this water soothe you let hope bring you a new life

this too shall pass

christian del pino

love yourself

in darkness

and in light

we will make it out alive

Made in the USA
Columbia, SC
03 April 2020

90486913R00119